DATE DUE

WHAT IS A TREE?

What is a
TREE?

by JENIFER W. DAY

illustrated by MANABU C. SAITO

gb GOLDEN PRESS • NEW YORK
Western Publishing Company, Inc., Racine, Wisconsin

TABLE OF CONTENTS

Conifers. 6

Palms. 8

Nuts. 10

The Birch and Others. 12

Oaks. 14

Magnolias. 16

The Rose Family .18

Legumes. 20

Maples. 22

Cactus Trees. 24

All Kinds of Trees. 26

The Ginkgo 28

Word List. 30

Note to Parents and Teachers. 32

This is a pine tree.
A pine tree has a woody trunk
    with rough bark.
A pine tree has many branches
    with needles.
A pine tree has roots.
A pine tree is a conifer.

A conifer is an evergreen tree.
A conifer is a tree that has scaly cones
    with seeds.
There are many kinds of conifers.

Juniper

Redwood

Douglas Fir

Balsam Fir

This is a coconut palm tree.
It has a tall trunk
    with smooth bark,
    and long feathery leaves.
Its fruit is good to eat.

There are many kinds of palm trees.
Most palm trees grow in the tropics.
Some have fan-like leaves.
Some have feathery leaves.
But all of them have green leaves.

Royal Palm

Date Palm

Thatch Palm

This
is a black
walnut tree.
It has a woody trunk
with rough bark.
It has branches
with green leaves.
It has roots under the ground.
Its nuts are good to eat.

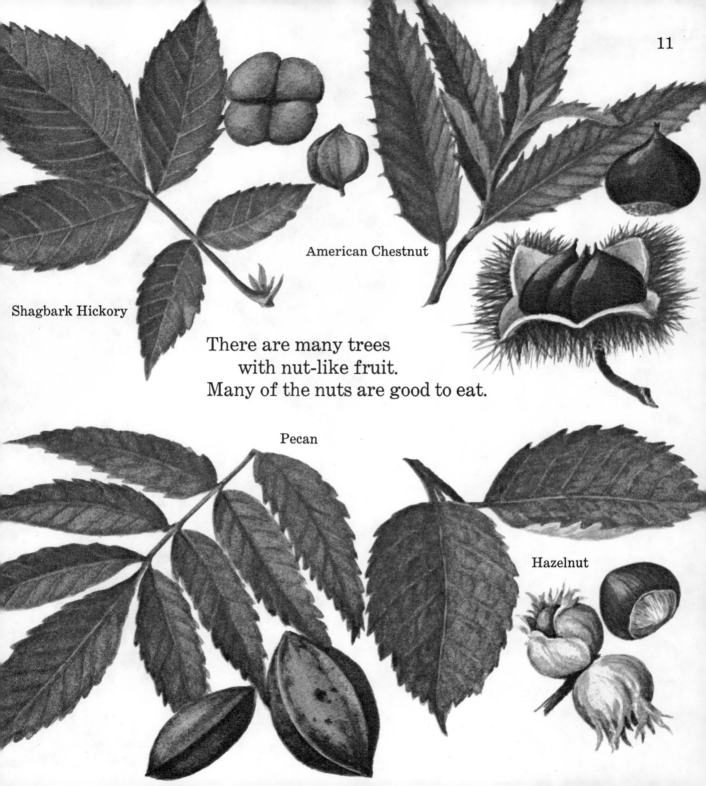

American Chestnut

Shagbark Hickory

There are many trees
with nut-like fruit.
Many of the nuts are good to eat.

Pecan

Hazelnut

This is a white birch.
It has a branched trunk
    with papery bark.
It has many branches
    with broad leaves.
It has roots under the ground.
A white birch is often planted
    for its beauty.

Tulip Tree

Black Willow

Trees may have single trunks
or branched trunks.
Trees may have slender leaves or
broad leaves or thorny leaves
or shiny leaves or fuzzy leaves.
But all trees have green leaves.

American Holly

Sassafras

This is a white oak tree.
It has a woody trunk
    with scaly bark.
It has many branches
    with broad green leaves.
It has deep roots in the ground.
Its fruit is an acorn.

Red Oak

Chinkapin Oak

There are many kinds of oak trees.
All of them have acorns.

Water Oak

Black Oak

Southern
Magnolia

This is a magnolia tree.
It has evergreen leaves,
 that are shiny on the top
 and fuzzy underneath.
It has big sweet-smelling flowers.

There are many kinds of magnolia trees.
Some are evergreen trees.
Some shed their leaves in winter.

Soulangeana

Sweet Bay

Cucumber Tree

Star
Magnolia

This is an apple tree.
An apple tree has
   sweet-smelling blossoms,
   and sweet-tasting fruit.
An apple tree is a member of the
   rose family.

Plum

Cherry

Pear

Peach

Plums and cherries belong
to the rose family.
Peaches and pears belong
to the rose family.
There are many members
in the rose family.

This is a honey locust.
It has a trunk with dark brown bark.
It has thorny branches with green leaves.
It has long, reddish seed pods.
A honey locust is a legume.

Redbud

Coral Bean

Some tree legumes are evergreen.
Some tree legumes shed their leaves.
But all legumes have seed pods.
There are many kinds of legumes.

Mesquite

Mescal Bean

This is a sugar maple tree.
It has a woody trunk
    covered with rough bark.
It has many branches
    and broad green leaves.
The green leaves change
    color in the autumn,
    and fall off in winter.
We get sugar from a
    sugar maple tree.

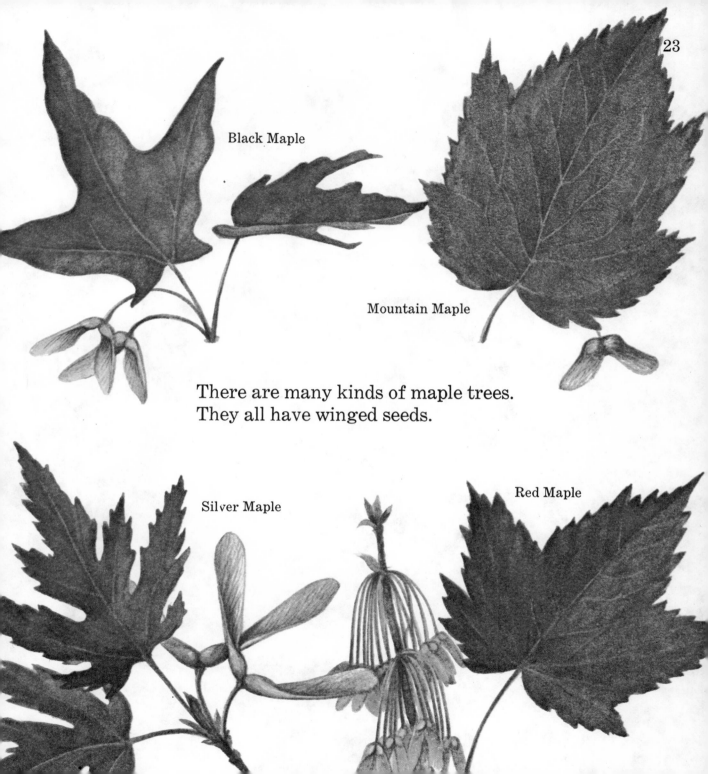

Black Maple

Mountain Maple

There are many kinds of maple trees.
They all have winged seeds.

Silver Maple

Red Maple

Saguaro

A cactus tree is a strange kind of tree.
It may have one trunk with many stems,
     or it may have only stems.
Its leaves are spiny needles.
Its flowers are bright colored.

Organ-pipe

Tree Cholla

Prickly Pear

This is a ginkgo tree.
It has fan-shaped leaves that
    turn bright yellow in the fall.
It is the only tree of its kind.

Trees grow in many places.
They grow in our yards
    and along city streets.
Trees grow in our parks
    and in our orchards.
They grow in the valleys
    and on mountaintops.
Sometimes a tree grows all alone.
But best of all, trees grow in forests
    all over the world.

There are many kinds of trees.
There are many sizes of trees.
There are evergreen trees, and trees
    that shed their leaves in winter.
There are trees with smooth bark,
    rough bark, scaly bark, shaggy bark,
    and papery bark.
We get many things from trees.
But, what is a tree?

A tree is a plant.
A tree is a plant that has a woody trunk
    covered with bark.
A tree is a plant that has many branches
    and green leaves.
A tree is a plant that has flowers, fruits
    and seeds.
A tree is a plant with roots underground.
A tree is the biggest plant of all.

WORD LIST

WORDS THAT NAME

acorn	conifer	needles	rose
apple	family	nuts	seed pods
autumn	flowers	oak	seeds
bark	fruit	one	stems
birch	ginkgo	palm	sugar
branches	ground	peaches	sugar maple
cactus	honey locust	pears	tree
cherries	leaves	pine	tropics
coconut palm	legumes	plant	trunk
color	magnolia	plums	walnut
cones	member	roots	winter

WORDS THAT DESCRIBE

beauty	fan-like	papery	spiny
biggest	fan-shaped	reddish	strange
black	feathery	rough	sweet-smelling
branched	fuzzy	scaly	sweet-tasting
bright	good	shaggy	tall
broad	green	shiny	thorny
brown	kinds	single	underground
colored	long	sizes	white
dark	many	slender	winged
deep	nut-like	smooth	woody
evergreen	only	some	yellow

ACTION WORDS

are	fall	has	planted
belong	get	have	shed
change	grow	is	turn

NOTE TO PARENTS AND TEACHERS

Children today are faced with a knowledge explosion unprecedented in recorded time. It is forcing parents, educators, and publishers to reexamine the kinds of books we place at their disposal. We must take shortcuts to expedite and expand their level of understanding. For that reason, this book, which is one of a series, has been designed as a beginner's introduction to concept development.

Trees are among the largest and oldest of all living things, but they make up only one group out of more than 350,000 kinds of plants. Because of anatomical and behavioral similarities and differences, every living thing has been classified to reflect the biological relationships of each. This book introduces, in a very elementary way, the notion of classification by using a representative sampling of different groups of trees. Each species illustrated is identified by its common name. At the same time the differences among species are being displayed, there is a continuity developed through a repetition of those characteristics held in common by all trees. A tree is identified as being a plant having certain basic characteristics, no matter how different one is from another.

This simple introduction to trees may initiate an early awareness of their importance in our environment.

While there has been no attempt to restrict the vocabulary to conform to standard readability levels, there has been an attempt to repeat words often enough to develop word recognition, even among the very young. It is supposed that this book may be used with children who are, as yet, non-readers. It is the philosophy of the author that many children suffer from mental retardation engendered by an all too common malady—lack of exposure. For that reason, there has been a deliberate introduction of words not usually found in books for this age level, but only those words needed to convey the concepts of diversity and uniformity among living things. It is to be assumed that any word that is understood orally may be learned visually, especially if it is encountered often enough to make an indelible impression.

The word list found on pages 30-31 has been included for those of you who wish to help some child practice word recognition out of context. The words have been divided into three groups according to the way they have been used in the text. Not all words used have been listed. At no time is it suggested that the use of the word list be extended beyond the child's own interest in learning the words included. It is simply an optional memory exercise.